The Hot Book

Dr Mike Goldsmith
Miranda Smith

RED SHED

First published in Great Britain 2015 by Red Shed,
an imprint of Egmont UK Limited
The Yellow Building, 1 Nicholas Road,
London W11 4AN

www.egmont.co.uk

Text copyright © Egmont UK Limited 2015

ISBN 978 1 4052 7403 6

Consultancy by Dr Patricia Macnair and Ryan Marek.

A CIP catalogue record for this book is available from the British Library.

The publisher would like to thank the following for permission to reproduce their material.
Every care has been taken to trace copyright holders. However, if there have been
unintentional omissions or failure to trace copyright holders, we apologize and will,
if informed, endeavour to make corrections in any future edition.

(OFC = Outside Front Cover, OBC = Outside Back Cover, b = bottom, c = centre, l = left, r = right, t = top)

2–3, 46–47 fluke samed/Shutterstock; OFC, 4 Zhu Difeng/Shutterstock; 6–7 Olga Nikonova/Shutterstock;
8bl Ammit Jack/Shutterstock; 8cl Pichugin Dmitry/Shutterstock; 8tl topseller/Shutterstock; 8br Talvi/Shutterstock;
8tr, 19c, 40–41c solarseven/Shutterstock; 9bl, 41cr Jana Schoenknecht/Shutterstock; 9br, 41br Maks Narodenko/
Shutterstock; 10bl EpicStockMedia/Shutterstock; 10tr, 40–41b Viahuta/Shutterstock.com; 11bl Hellen Sergeyeva/
Shutterstock; 11br G. Light/Shutterstock; 11cr FotograFFF/Shutterstock; 11tr Roman Sigaev/Shutterstock;
12br Peshkova/Shutterstock; 12cl, 12cr, 13cl, 13cr Ostill/Shutterstock; 13br Image Point Fr/Shutterstock;
13tr Andrey Burmakin/Shutterstock; 14bl Peter Waters/Shutterstock; 14br Takahashi Photography/Shutterstock;
14c Lara Zanarini/Shutterstock; 14cl Michael Sheehan/Shutterstock; 14tr Maxene Huiyu/Shutterstock; 15bl Mike
Buckley; 14–15c Lara Zanarini/Shutterstock; 15br Piotr Gatlik/Shutterstock; 15cr Mark Herreid/Shutterstock;
15tl Michael & Patricia Fogden/Getty Images; 15tr Wayne Lawler/Science Photo Library; 16–17c Webitect/
Shutterstock; 16c Dr. Joerg Szarzynski; 16bl Jixin YU/Shutterstock; 17br Georgette Douwma/naturepl.com;
17cr Phase4Studios/Shutterstock; 17tc Emilio Ereza/Alamy; 18bc Wil Meinderts/Buiten-beeld/Minden Pictures/
Getty Images; 18br Dea Picture Library/De Agostini/Getty Images; 18tr Heritage Image Partnership Ltd/Alamy;
18–19 photobess58/Shutterstock; 19bl Sonia Halliday Photographs/Alamy; 19cr Paulo M. F. Pires/Shutterstock;
19tr My Good Images/Shutterstock; 20b Melkor3D/Shutterstock; 20cl Lefteris Papaulakis/Shutterstock.com;
20tr Catmando/Shutterstock; 21br Fotokostic/Shutterstock; 21cl 123Nelson/Shutterstock; 21cr (head) Pindyurin
Vasily/Shutterstock; 21cr (body) LilKar/Shutterstock; 21tl Pakmor/Shutterstock; 22–23 phoelix/Shutterstock;
22bl Diana Taliun/Shutterstock; 22br Patrick Foto/Shutterstock; 22tc A.B. Dowsett/Science Photo Library;
22tl Brian A Jackson/Shutterstock; 23c Alena Brozova/Shutterstock; 23cl Leungchopan/Shutterstock; 23cr Dmitry
Kalinovsky/Shutterstock; 23tl CREATISTA/Shutterstock; 24bc Mopic/Shutterstock; 24c Designua/Shutterstock;
24–25c (volcano) Pablo Hidalgo – Fotos 593/Shutterstock; 24–25c (eruption) John David Bigl III/Shutterstock;
25cr OAR/NATIONAL UNDERSEA RESEARCH PROGRAM (NURP); NOAA; 25tl Alberto Garcia/Corbis; 25tr
Dmussman/Shutterstock; 26–27c Mint Images Limited/Alamy; 26bl Loskutnikov/Shutterstock; 26–27 Nagel
Photography/Shutterstock; 27cr (squirrel) Vladislav T. Jirousek/Shutterstock; 27br Juniors Bildarchiv GmbH/
Alamy; 27cr (beetle) Vblinov/Shutterstock; 27tr All Canada Photos/Alamy; 27tl, 29tl Vadimmmus/Shutterstock;
28bl blickwinkel/Alamy; 28–29c, 29cl Dr. Morley Read/Shutterstock; 29br Bluegreen Pictures/Alamy;
29cr, 40–41t Erik Zandboer/Shutterstock; 30tr Triff/Shutterstock; 30tl silver tiger/Shutterstock 30 (sunset)
MO_SESPremium/Shutterstock; 30 (ground) Sunny Forest/Shutterstock; 30 (tree) Ni Haosheng/Shutterstock;
31l Piotr Krzeslak/Shutterstock; 31bl AFP/Getty Images; 31br Jim Reed/Science Photo Library; 31cr Reed Timmer
& Jim Bishop/Science Photo Library; 32b Hung Chung Chih/Shutterstock.com; 32c Benoit Daoust/Shutterstock;
32bc Lightspring/Shutterstock; 33bl US Air Force – digital version c Science Faction/Corbis; 33bc Aleksey
Stemmer/Shutterstock; 33c Bayanova Svetlana/Shutterstock; 33cr, 40bl Levent Konuk/Shutterstock;
33tl FloridaStock/Shutterstock; 34–35c Lordprice Collection/Alamy; 34b GUSTOIMAGES/Science Photo Library;
35b Chriss73/Shutterstock; 35tl Martin Bond/Science Photo Library; 35tr Mark Scott/Shutterstock.com; 36–37c
solarseven/Shutterstock; 36bl Stocktrek Images, Inc./Alamy; 36tl NASA/JPL – Caltech/ZMASS; 37br NASA/
ESA, J. Hester, A Loll (ASU); 37tr Tristan3D/Shutterstock; 38r highviews/Shutterstock; 38l Luiz Antonio da Silva/
Shutterstock; 39bl Scientifica/Visuals Unlimited, Inc./Science Photo Library; 39br Igor Zh/Shutterstock; 39cl Arena
Photo UK/Shutterstock; 39cr, 41tr scyther5/Shutterstock; 39tl Jiang Hongyan/Shutterstock; 39tr The Oxfordshire
Chilli Garden/Alamy; 42–43 Ulza/Shutterstock; 44–45 Skydie/Shutterstock; OBC All shutterstock. All textures and
illustrated elements are courtesy of Shutterstock.

Contents

Hot, hot, hot!

Without heat we would not survive for long. How much heat there is in the bodies of all living things affects the efficiency with which they work. Heat is needed to grow and prepare food; heat affects the planet's weather; and heat plays a vital role in making things that we use every day.

Heat is measured by temperature. Objects that have a high temperature we describe as hot. We cannot see heat, but we can feel it and see its effects: we see air shimmering above a hot road; feel the heat coming from a candle flame; see grass turning brown in a hot, dry summer. Our planet runs on heat that comes from deep inside its molten core as well as from our star, the Sun. Throughout the universe, heat is constantly being generated, changed and used. Heat is everywhere – and sometimes in surprising places!

The science of heat

Heat is a kind of energy that is present in all matter, and heat energy constantly flows into and out of all objects, moving energy from a higher temperature to a lower temperature. Heat energy can be harnessed to do useful and efficient work – factories use it to make everyday materials and engines burn fuels to power machines.

ENERGY

There are many different kinds of energy and they can change from one kind to another. For example, the food you eat contains chemical energy that is partly changed into heat energy during digestion to keep your body warm. The hotter something is, the faster the molecules in it move as its heat energy increases. Without energy everything comes to a halt.

To stop a car, the brakes must turn the car's kinetic energy into heat energy. This is done by the brake pads clamping down on the brake discs and using friction to generate heat.

FRICTION

Friction happens when any two objects rub against or slide past one another. Friction always slows down a moving object, so when two objects lose speed in this way, they have to release energy, and they do this in the form of heat energy. You can feel this when you rub your cold hands together and they get warmer.

Surfers benefit from the friction between the bottom of a wave and the seafloor. The lower part of the wave heats up and slows down, while the upper part continues to travel at speed, rising up and curling before breaking on the shore. The froth at the top of the wave also provides friction that heats the wave.

HOW HEAT TRAVELS

Heat always moves from a hot object to a cold one until their temperatures equalize. How fast heat does this depends on the difference in temperature between the two objects and how easily the heat can move.

Convection is the transfer of heat through the movement of a liquid such as water, or a gas such as air. The water in this pot is being heated by the flames and transferring heat upwards towards the surface and then up into the air.

Radiation is the transfer of heat by electromagnetic (light and heat) waves through the air. This gas flame is radiating heat upwards and outwards, to warm the pan and the air around it.

Conduction is the transfer of heat from one molecule to another in a substance. The heat travels from the gas flame and through the glass container into the water.

DID YOU KNOW?

Your computer would be slow and overheat without its heat sink. It cools down the computer by conducting heat away from the central processing unit (CPU) into fins that have a large surface area and can spread the hot air through the rest of the computer. A fan blows out excess hot air.

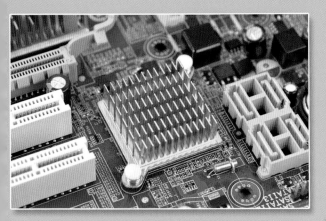

The microprocessor on this computer circuit board is cooled by the heat sink (centre) that sits on top of it. Heat sinks are usually made of a metal that's a good conductor of heat.

GETTING BIGGER

Most solids, liquids and gases expand when they are heated because, when their molecules move faster, they bump into each other and move further apart. Steam engines, rockets and car engines are all powered by the expansion of gases.

Expanded gas blasts out of the rocket and provides a thrust to propel the rocket in the other direction.

People and heat

Your body makes heat all the time – when your heart beats, when your muscles move, when you digest food, even when you think! And it is very good at keeping its average internal temperature at a steady 37°C. The human body has also evolved ways of coping when the weather is hot or when it is attacked by a virus. But it is less good at coping with the scorching effects of the Sun.

BLOOD AND SWEAT

When you exercise, blood collects heat as it passes through your muscles. The blood carries this heat to the skin, travelling through a network of blood vessels to just under the skin's surface. When your body is in danger of overheating, these vessels widen to allow more blood to reach the surface and lose heat to the air more quickly.

Most of the time, the air around you carries away heat from your skin. However, if this does not cool you enough, you start to sweat. The sweat evaporates from the hot skin, cooling it down.

HEATING UP

When you are too cold, the blood vessels in the skin contract, or narrow, so that blood flow to the skin is reduced and your body retains heat. You may start shivering, which is an involuntary, rapid contraction of the muscles. This extra muscle activity generates more heat and warms you up.

RUNNING A TEMPERATURE

Viruses and bacteria have evolved to work best at our core temperature of 37°C, so when your body is attacked, it fights back by raising your temperature. This stops a virus multiplying and causes it to die. So running a temperature – as long as it does not go too high – can be a good sign!

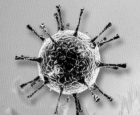

A small amount of sunlight does us good – for example, it helps us to make vitamin D. But it does not take much more to damage us. So our skins contain cells called melanocytes, whose job it is to produce melanin. Melanin traps sunlight so that it does not reach the deep layers of the skin and do damage there. The more melanin a person's skin contains, the darker brown they are.

The toughest marathon on Earth is the Badwater Ultramarathon through Death Valley in California, where the temperature reaches 55°C. Athletes prepare by sweating it out in saunas.

The average person has 2.6 million sweat glands in their skin.

BURNING HOT

Our skins are equipped with very sensitive heat-detecting nerve endings, which mean we know almost instantly if we are touching something hot. We also have a built-in reaction called a reflex that is very quick – for instance, you automatically pull your hand away from a hot flame before you even think about it. Sometimes the heat is so great that damage is done before you can pull away and you get burned.

WHEN HEAT WINS

If your body cannot keep cool enough, the result is heat exhaustion. Sufferers become weak and dizzy, with pounding hearts, low blood pressure and hot, dry skin. It is vital to cool down and drink plenty of fluid.

Cold   Hot

Animals
in the heat

Living in very hot conditions is a challenge for many animals. Most limit their activity to times of the day when it is cooler. Some burrow, or hide in the shade of rocks and vegetation. Many sweat because drying sweat cools the skin. But some animals have even more ingenious ways of beating the heat.

LICKING
Kangaroos lick their arms until they are covered in saliva. When a breeze blows across their wet arms, the saliva evaporates. This carries away body heat and cools the animal.

EATING POO
Some dung beetles make a ball of animal poo and roll it away. For the rest of their lives, they do not need to eat or drink anything but the dung, which means that they can live in very hot and dry conditions.

The beetles lay their eggs in the dung ball, so the grubs have instant food and drink!

Vultures wee on their legs to keep cool!

When a hive gets too warm, a special bee team keeps cool air flowing by flapping their wings in the same direction.

Costa's hummingbirds travel to stay cool. They breed in winter in the desert areas of northern Mexico. As the hot summer months begin, they set off for the cooler coastal areas further north, sometimes as far away as Alaska.

The shovel-snouted lizard runs over hot desert sand very fast. This short contact with the hot surface means it avoids getting toasted feet!

WATER STORAGE

In Australian summers, the water-holding frog drinks until it is bloated, covers itself in slime and buries itself in the desert sand. It can stay underground like this for up to two years.

PANTING

Dogs and cats don't sweat, except for the undersides of their paws. Dogs lose heat by panting or staying in the shade. Cats flatten themselves out on a cool surface. Some cats have thick coats to shade them from the sun.

African elephants are the largest land mammals on Earth.

RADIATING

The huge ears of an elephant provide the extra skin needed to radiate away heat. The smaller an animal is, the more skin it has for its volume. So a mouse can get rid of excess heat much more easily than an elephant.

FIERY FACT

The deep-sea Pompeii worm is the most heat-tolerant animal on Earth. It lives near hydrothermal vents in water temperatures of up to 80°C.

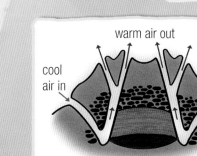

warm air out

cool air in

cool air in

AIR-CONDITIONED

In a termite nest, air shafts at the base of the mound allow cooling air to flow in. Warm air rises up and out through shafts at the top. This maintains a constant temperature of 30°C for the gardens of fungi that the termites farm for food.

Plants *and* heat

Unlike animals, many plants can survive even if they become very hot. However, they wilt and fade in bright sunlight and waterless conditions, and they can be destroyed by fire, so some species have evolved special ways to beat the heat. Some extraordinary plants are even able to raise their internal temperature, using the extra heat to send out scents that attract insects.

HOT STUFF!

The world's largest flower, the titan arum, gets itself noticed by pumping clouds of stench into the night sky. It sends waves of heat up through the flower until the tip reaches 36°C. Then the flower opens enough to release a cloud of stinking steam. The smell of rotting flesh attracts various insects that pollinate the plant. The plant flowers for only two days and nights.

A SPIKY DEFENCE

All plants must take in and give out water, and they do this mostly through their leaves. Cacti, which almost all grow in hot, dry places, have spikes that lose much less water than normal leaves. The spikes also protect the cactus from thirsty animals that might suck out water.

This thermal image of the titan arum, also known as the corpse flower, shows the plant heating up – orange and red are the hottest temperatures.

The leaves of the African Welwitschia plant are dead for much of their length, with only the parts nearest the stem growing very slowly all the time. These special leaves are shaped so that the dew that collects on them at dawn and dusk trickles down to the roots.

The Mexican Old Man cactus is covered in a reflective layer of white 'hair' that protects it from frost and the sun.

HIDDEN WINDOWS

The South African stone plant looks more like a pebble than a living thing. Most of the plant is buried in the top layer of desert sand. The only visible part is a 'window' that lets in light onto the hidden leaf surfaces. The stone plant can open or close this window to avoid overheating.

FIRE TREES

Australian eucalyptus trees have not only adapted to fire but actually benefit from it! Eucalyptus oil is highly flammable, and the fallen leaves and peeling bark combined with leaf litter can turn a small ground fire into a terrifying inferno. After the fire has swept through, the tree has seed capsules that open once they are burned, so the eucalyptus has a head start on regrowth.

LIFE AFTER DEATH

Some plants benefit from being burned! The South African fire lily grows only after a forest fire has swept through, burning everything in its path. The lily flourishes because this is the only time when there are no other plants around to compete with it for water, light or space.

Fire-breather Antonio Restivo blew a flame 8.05m high on 11 January 2011.

Fire

Of all the things that people have discovered, fire is one of the most important. No one knows when this happened, but ash has been found in Wonderwerk Cave, South Africa, suggesting that people there used fire to cook more than a million years ago. Through the ages, people have discovered many different uses for fire.

30,000 ya
CAVE PAINTINGS

Ancient peoples decorated walls of caves with paint made from the charcoal of heated wood. This was mixed with spit or animal fat.

800 BCE
IRON AGE

People learned how to extract iron from rocks by smelting (see page 23). They used bellows to blow fresh air onto flames and reach a higher temperature.

475 mya
FIRST FIRE

There were no fires on Earth until about 475 mya because there were few plants on the planet. Plants produce a gas called oxygen, without which no fire can burn.

Early fires would have been started by lightning striking dry vegetation from trees very similar to this gingko.

Iron Age spears

FIERY FACT

Firefighters wear clothing made with Kevlar to protect themselves against the intense heat from a fire. Kevlar was invented in 1965 by US chemist Stephanie Kwolek.

WHAT IS FIRE?

Fire is the result of a chemical reaction called combustion, the scientific name for burning. When a fuel such as coal or wood burns, parts of it combine with oxygen in the air. This produces new gases, releasing heat and light as flames.

6CE
FIRE BRIGADE

The first fire brigade was established in Rome. It consisted of 7,000 firefighters called *vigils*.

1110
FIREWORKS

A grand firework display was put on for Emperor Huizong of Song in China in 1110. The first fireworks were bamboo shoots filled with gunpowder.

2009
WILDFIRES

The Black Saturday bushfires blazed across Victoria, Australia, in February 2009. Millions of animals and 173 people were killed, and more than 445,000 hectares of land were destroyed.

672CE
GREEK FIRE

This weapon is said to have been invented by Callinicus of Heliopolis. A stream of burning liquid – probably containing sulphur or quicklime – was capable of destroying an enemy fleet.

1826
FIRST MATCH

English chemist John Walker discovered by accident that a stick coated with chemicals bursts into flames when scraped across the hearth. He had invented the match!

Legends of fire and heat

To many people through the ages fire seemed to have magical properties – it moved and grew, it ate fuel but it could be killed by water. Staring into a fire, they could see strange shapes that fed their fearful imaginations. Fiery myths and legends were born in those flickering flames.

In Chinese mythology, the phoenix ate only dewdrops.

FLAME BIRD

It was said that every thousand years, the phoenix would burn up in the Sun's rays, and from the ashes a new bird would rise. For the ancient Egyptians and Greeks, the phoenix symbolized immortality. In Arabian myth, it sang a song so enchanting that even the Sun god stopped to listen. Today, a person who makes a comeback is said to be 'rising like a phoenix'.

FIRE FROM A GOD

Ancient Greeks told the story of Prometheus, who gave the secret of fire-making to men and was sentenced to a terrible punishment. He was chained to a rock and every day an eagle ate his liver. During the night, the liver would grow back, ready for the eagle to start again the next morning.

BREATH OF FIRE

There are legends of dragons all round the world. They are often described as huge lizard-like monsters that fly, breathe fire and like to curl up on a mound of treasure. In China, many people believe that they descend from dragons, which they worship as a force for good. Chinese dragons are powerful, strong and bring good luck to those who deserve it.

Some cultures believe that dragons control water, rain, floods and hurricanes.

BORN OF FIRE

The salamander is a shy amphibian. But for many the 'fire lizard' was a creature that lived its entire life in fire. In India and Europe during the Middle Ages, a material said to be the solidified breath or hair of the salamander was used to protect precious objects from fire. We now know that the material they used was asbestos, a real fireproof material.

Salamanders were thought to emerge from volcanoes and have the power to control fire.

MONSTERS FROM THE EAST

In Arabia, there are many ruins left behind by long-vanished civilizations. In the past, people avoided these places because they thought they contained a race of monsters called efreets. Although not all efreets were bad – some even married humans – many of them were as cruel as they were powerful.

Efreets were said to be giant, winged creatures made from fire.

FIERY FACT

Dancers perform the Chinese dragon dance during Chinese New Year and other festivals. The longer the dragon, the more luck it is thought to bring.

LAVA CREATURE

Chile is a country rich in volcanoes, and according to local legends, at least one is inhabited by a giant monster called Cherufe. Not only can Cherufe live in molten lava, it is actually made of it. Unfortunately for local villagers, Cherufe is as happy outside its volcano as in. What's more, without Cherufe inside to keep it quiet, it is said that the volcano will erupt.

Cherufe enjoys eating people, cooking them as it does so.

Uses of heat

As heat increases and temperature rises, the behaviour of materials changes, and so do the bodies of living things. Over the years, scientists have learned the reasons for these changes. They have applied this knowledge to find ways to use different levels of heat to solve many practical problems.

OVER 60°C PASTEURIZATION

Pasteurization is used to kill germs. Food is heated carefully and for a short time to just the right temperature to kill germs without changing the taste of the food.

200°C IRONING

Ironing works because the heat of the iron affects the tiny fibres that clothes are made of. The heat removes tiny amounts of trapped electricity and also softens the material so that its fibres do not stick together.

25–30°C BROODING

Newborn chicks need to be kept warm for the first six weeks of their lives. Farmers do this with special infrared brooding lamps. The infrared heat passes through the air without heating it. When it reaches the chick, the heat energy is absorbed.

100°C FLYING HIGH

If a balloon is filled with air and this is heated, the air will expand. The balloon will not be able to hold it all, so some of the air will escape. The balloon will now weigh less than the air around it and it will rise.

600°C GLASS BLOWING

Heat melts many substances. Some, such as glass, soften before becoming liquid. If air is blown into a lump of heated glass (*left*), it can be shaped into a bottle or vase, before being allowed to cool and harden into that shape.

The temperature of the surface of the Sun is about 5,600°C.

3,100°C WELDING

If two pieces of metal are held together and heated, parts of them will turn into thick liquids. They weld, or mix, together. If the heat is then removed, the liquid metals will turn back into a solid lump that joins the two pieces of metal.

340°C REFINING

To separate crude oil into many useful substances, such as petrol, it is slowly heated in oil refineries. Different liquids run off at different temperatures, finally leaving behind a thick, sticky substance called bitumen.

1,540°C SMELTING

The metal we use most is iron, which can be moulded or beaten into any shape. Iron is found in rocks that are coloured red by the presence of the metal. The rocks are heated until the iron melts in a process called smelting. The iron is poured into a mould to cool and use.

FIERY FACT

The hottest and driest place in North America is Death Valley, California. The highest recorded temperature in the world, 56.7°C, was recorded there on 10 July 1913.

Fiery Earth

If you were able to drill down 6,400km to the centre of Earth, you would find temperatures of around 6,700°C. This internal heat provides energy for our dynamic planet. It pushes parts of Earth's crust around, moving continents, building mountains and causing volcanoes to erupt.

MOVING CONTINENTS

Earth's surface is broken up into tectonic plates. These float on top of magma (molten rock) and move against one another because of heat currents in the mantle. When the plates meet they may crash together, pull apart or scrape past each other. This activity often causes strong earthquakes or volcanoes.

Earth's solid crust is broken up into about eight major tectonic plates and many minor ones. Volcanoes are most likely to occur along the boundaries between the plates.

HEAT STORAGE

Most heat inside Earth is stored in the mantle. Some heat remains from when the planet began to form over 4.6 billion years ago. There is heat from friction caused by denser material sinking and pushing less dense material outwards. But up to 90 per cent is produced by elements such as uranium, potassium and thorium decaying and radiating heat as they offload excess energy.

Crust
Mantle
Liquid outer core
Solid inner core
Surface

There are about **1,500** active volcanoes **worldwide.**

Mount Pinatubo erupted in 1991 after lying dormant for 500 years.

HOT SPRINGS

There are many hot springs all over the world. Most are formed from surface water that has seeped underground, been heated there and returned to the surface. In some cases, the water is heated by very hot volcanic rock that is quite close to the surface.

In sub-zero temperatures, Japanese macaques soak in the warmth of a volcanic hot spring.

DID YOU KNOW?

Scientists study volcanoes to further our understanding of the deep Earth and also so that they can warn people if there is likely to be an eruption. They measure the movement or shaking underground – seismicity – as well as changes in gases or the shape of a volcano. The strengths are measured on the Volcanic Explosivity Index (VEI) on a scale of 0 (the smallest) to 8 (the largest).

The water is full of particles of minerals such as sulphur, copper and zinc.

EARTH'S MOST POWERFUL VOLCANOES

Yellowstone, USA
640,000 years ago VEI 8

Mount Tambora, Sumbawa, Indonesia
1815 VEI 7

Krakatoa, Indonesia
1883 VEI 6

Mount Pinatubo, Luzon, Philippines
1991 VEI 6

Mount St Helens, USA
1980 VEI 5

Lascar, Chile
1993 VEI 4

RAINING FIRE

At this very moment, between 15 and 20 volcanoes are erupting around the world, as magma forces its way up from a chamber deep underground. Of the 1,500 active volcanoes, the biggest are the stratovolcanoes. When these erupt, they blast ash and gas high into the atmosphere where they travel for thousands of kilometres.

BLACK SMOKERS

Deep in the ocean, there are areas of the sea floor where water heated by volcanic activity gushes out in black clouds. The water temperature can reach over 400°C. These hydrothermal vents are home to unique plants and animals that have evolved to flourish in the warmth.

Desert heat

A desert is an area where there is less than 25cm of rainfall in a year, but some deserts actually get less than 25mm! Despite this lack of water, deserts are remarkably rich in plant and animal life that has adapted to live in harsh conditions (see also pages 14–17).

HOT DESERTS

Deserts cover almost a third of our planet's surface and are found on every continent. Most of them are hot deserts that are on either side of the Equator around the Tropic of Cancer and the Tropic of Capricorn. What little water these hot deserts receive is lost almost immediately through evaporation.

LIVING IN THE DESERT

Most desert-dwellers live in small villages, some of which are next to fertile oases, so they can grow crops. Many people have to walk many kilometres each day to the nearest well to fetch water. Other desert peoples live a nomadic life, travelling with their herds and goods to springs or wells.

WATER ILLUSION

In the desert, people are often misled by the reflections of the sky off thin layers of hot air near the heated ground. They think they can see an area of water in the distance. This optical illusion is called a mirage.

SINGING DUNES

In the Sahara, the desert wind pushes sand up towards the top of large, crescent-shaped dunes called barchans. When the angle reaches a tipping point of 35°, rivers of sand slide downwards, filling the air with a deep humming sound, like the engine of a plane, that can be heard up to 10km away. Different dunes sing different notes.

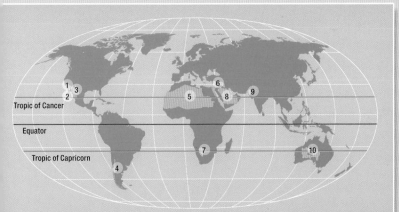

Top 10 Hottest Deserts:

1 Mojave
2 Sonoran
3 Chihuahuan
4 Monte
5 Sahara
6 Syrian
7 Kalahari
8 Arabian
9 Thar
10 Australian

DID YOU KNOW?

Animals and plants have evolved some intriguing techniques for survival in hot deserts.

Many, like this kangaroo rat, are nocturnal, only emerging from cool underground burrows at night to hunt for food.

Women expertly balance clay vessels full of water on their heads in the Thar desert of India and Pakistan. The women collect water daily from a well and carry it back 10km in the scorching heat to their villages.

The darkling beetle collects moisture on its body from early morning fogs and drinks it as it trickles down.

The Cape ground squirrel has a flattened tail nearly as long as its body, and shelters under it in the heat of the day.

1.6%
of the world's population lives in hot deserts.

The sand moves downhill at 40m/s, with sand grains colliding about 100 times a second. This turns the face of the dune into a huge loudspeaker.

The honey mesquite of the Sonoran desert has a tap root up to 58m long to draw water up from deep in the ground.

Tropical rainforests

Tropical rainforests are some of the warmest places on Earth. In their hot and humid climates it rains nearly every day, and the temperatures fluctuate only a few degrees through the year. These forests are perfect habitats for more than half of the world's plant and animal species because there are no shortages of food.

HOT RAINFORESTS

Less than seven per cent of Earth's surface is covered in tropical rainforests. These are all close to the Equator where temperatures are high all year round, and there are average monthly temperatures of more than 25°C.

Plants in the **Amazon** rainforest produce more than **20%** of the world's **oxygen.**

DAILY WEATHER

Tropical rainforests produce their own weather cycles. In the morning, the sun shines and heats up the forest, causing hot, wet air to rise through the trees and condense to form cumulus clouds above the canopy. In the afternoon, the clouds release rain that filters back down to the forest floor and the whole cycle begins again.

WARMED BY THE SUN

The trees are always green because there are no seasons, so they grow all the time. The sunlight absorbed by their leaves is converted into chemical energy through the process of photosynthesis. The plants store huge amounts of carbon, releasing oxygen into the atmosphere.

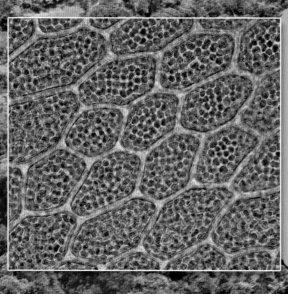

This cross-section of a leaf shows the round, green chloroplasts that absorb sunlight during photosynthesis.

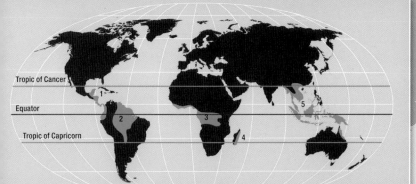

Tropic of Cancer

Equator

Tropic of Capricorn

1 Central America rainforest
2 Amazon rainforest
3 Congo river basin rainforest
4 Madagascar rainforest
5 Southeast Asia rainforest

FALLING FOXES

Increased global warming (see pages 32–33) is threatening many rainforest species. On 12 January 2002, in Australia, temperatures soared to 42.9°C – eight degrees higher than usual. Flying foxes, which doze in the treetops during the day, began to pant and lick their wrists in an attempt to cool themselves. Then they fell from the trees dead.

In total, between 2003 and 2006, heatwaves killed more than 20,000 flying foxes.

LIVING ON AIR

Many plants have adaptations to allow them to flourish in the heat. Epiphytes have adapted to grow in the upper canopy to get as much sunlight as possible. They live on the branches of trees, taking their moisture and nutrients from the air.

DRIP TIP

Thick, leathery and shiny leaves protect trees against both sunlight and rainfall. Many plants have leaves that are grooved or have long, thin drip spouts that help water slip off, keeping the leaves dry and stopping mould and mildew from forming.

Hot weather

A layer of mixed gases about 800km deep – the atmosphere – surrounds Earth and stops it from becoming too hot or too cold for life. All weather happens in the troposphere, the layer of the atmosphere nearest the planet's surface. Heat energy from the Sun is spread around our planet in the troposphere via winds, clouds and rain.

BALANCING ACT

As light and heat from the Sun enter the atmosphere, some is immediately reflected back into space. The rest goes through the atmosphere and is absorbed by Earth's surface. The Earth is round, so the Sun strikes some places more directly. The more direct sunlight is, the more intense and hot it is.

The Sun shines directly onto the Equator so it is very hot there. It shines at an angle onto the North and South poles, so it is colder there.

EXTREME HEAT

Long periods of heat can cause disasters. Animals and plants die and people are driven out of their homes. And it takes only a spark to start a wildfire in a drought area. Winds can cause the rapid spread of such fires by carrying burning embers to new areas.

Yuma, in Arizona, USA, has an average of 4,055 hours of sunshine in a year!

HOT LIGHTNING

Lightning is an electric current and not hot in itself. But it travels at more than 220,000km/h, causing the air it passes through to heat to an extraordinary 28,000°C – five times hotter than the surface of the Sun! The air is heated so quickly that the molecules expand and explode, creating the loud noise we call thunder.

SPINNING WINDS

Hot weather fills the atmosphere with energy, sometimes leading to a tornado, in which warm air mixes with cold air and spins round at high speed. It drags up dust to form a funnel-like shape, which then drifts across the land at up to 110km/h, destroying everything in its path.

There are about **1,800 thunderstorms** around the globe **every day.**

DEADLY SANDSTORM

In some parts of the world, there are winds so fierce that they have their own names. One such wind is the simoon, which means 'poisonous wind'. It affects the deserts of north Africa and Arabia as well as nearby countries. It is very hot, dry and dusty.

Sandstorms happen when strong winds move over deserts, sucking up sand as they go. Sometimes sand is carried right across continents.

In summer, rising hot air in storm clouds called cumulonimbus can cause pieces of ice to circle up and down, growing as they do. They fall to Earth as hailstones that can be bigger than baseballs.

Global warming

Earth is getting warmer, but how do we know this and are we to blame? Scientists are measuring everything from carbon dioxide levels in the air to how many hectares of the rainforest are burned down each year, and how much sea levels have risen in parts of the world to establish what damage is being caused.

GREENHOUSE GASES

Greenhouse gases, such as water vapour, carbon dioxide, methane and ozone, in the atmosphere keep Earth at the right temperature for life by trapping some of the Sun's heat. But the concentration of these gases is increasing because of our actions, including the burning of fossil fuels and deforestation.

4% reflected by Earth's surface

6% scattered by the atmosphere

19% absorbed by the atmosphere

20% scattered and reflected by clouds

51% absorbed by Earth

CARBON OVERLOAD

We burn fossil fuels to create energy to heat our houses, fuel our cars, grow our food, and make things we use every day. Every time we burn these fuels, carbon dioxide is released into the atmosphere.

The pollution of the atmosphere by car exhausts causes many premature deaths.

Instead of planting more forests, many people are cutting them down for timber or farmland.

DEFORESTATION

Not only are we burning too many fossil fuels but we are destroying too many rainforests around the world. The balance between carbon dioxide production and absorption cannot be maintained (see pages 28–29), so Earth is in danger of becoming too warm.

EFFECTS

SOLUTIONS

Melting ice caps are changing life for polar bears. Without as much sea ice, swimming conditions are dangerous and there are fewer seals for them to hunt.

RENEWABLE ENERGY

It is important to find alternative energy sources to fossil fuels. Heat from the Sun can be harnessed to power homes. And the same heat causes the wind to blow for wind power, helps plants to grow for biomass energy, and causes evaporation and rainfall to make hydropower possible.

Wind turbines capture energy from the wind and use it to generate electricity that can be stored until it is needed.

OUR WORLD IN DANGER

The polar ice caps and glaciers are melting worldwide, causing sea levels to rise. This significantly affects people who live near the coast, as well as wildlife habitats. Warmer air may result in stormier weather and bigger hurricanes. Hotter air means more water evaporation and more rain, which could mean more flooding.

RECYCLING

When you recycle, you are reducing your carbon footprint – the amount of carbon that is emitted when something is made, transported and used. And it takes 95 per cent less energy to recycle a can than it does to make it from raw materials.

If you recycle one aluminium can, it saves enough energy to run a television for three hours!

BIOMASS ENERGY

Plants take carbon out of the atmosphere when they are growing and return it when they are burned. We need to replant forests that we have lost, and choose high-yield crops to use as alternative fuels.

In 2005, storm surges caused by Hurricane Katrina resulted in the devastating flooding of the city of New Orleans, USA.

We can grow plants such as sunflowers and soya beans to produce oil that can be used to make fuels.

Hot tech

People are very inventive. Over thousands of years, they have worked out ways to use things that they found, and modify objects that existed already. All inventions need energy (see page 10) to work, and heat is a popular source for that energy. Here are just six of those extraordinary inventions.

STEAM POWER

In a steam engine, fire heats water to produce steam, which, at high pressure, drives cylinders that power the engine. Steam engines have been used to power many things, including the first trains. Today, large steam turbines drive electric generators in power stations to produce more than 80 per cent of the world's electricity.

FLAME-THROWER

In the 7th century, the Byzantines fired flaming liquid at enemy ships (see page 19). The liquid was probably a mixture of pine resin, naptha and sulphur or quicklime (calcium oxide). During World War I (1914–1918), the modern flame-thrower with petrol or natural gas was used to project a long stream of fire at the enemy.

MICROWAVE OVEN

In 1947, the first commercial microwave oven was built. Inside, a magnetron generates radio waves. At a particular frequency, the radio waves (microwaves) agitate water molecules in food. The molecules vibrate, creating heat, which in turn cooks the food.

Magnetron

Glass plate

This X-ray shows food cooking in a microwave oven. The bowl is turning slowly on a glass plate as the microwaves cook the food to ensure that it heats evenly.

FIERY FACT

The invention of the microwave oven happened by accident. In 1945, Percy Spencer was experimenting with a new machine called a magnetron. He noticed that it melted the chocolate bar in his pocket and then tried out the magnetron near popcorn with great success.

This nuclear power station in Leibstadt is the largest in Switzerland and produces about one-sixth of all the electricity used in that country.

The wide heat shield bears the brunt as the spacecraft passes through the atmosphere at up to 10km/sec.

HEAT SHIELD

Heat shields on space capsules protect both the spacecraft and crew from the 2,200°C temperature that is produced on re-entry into Earth's atmosphere. The largest shield ever built has been tested ready for travel on NASA's Orion deep-space capsule, which from 2021 will carry crew to visit asteroids and Mars.

DIATHERMY

US engineer and inventor Nikola Tesla discovered in 1891 that it was possible to heat parts of the human body using a high-frequency electrical current. This 'diathermy' ('heating through') is now used for deep muscle and joint treatment. It can also be used as a part of surgery to destroy infection.

Today, as well as military deployment, flame-throwers are used by farmers for controlled burning of fields or by firefighters to burn off vegetation to stop wildfires.

SOLAR COOKER

In 1767, physicist Horace de Saussure used five layers of glass boxes turned upside down on a black table to cook fruit. Today's solar cookers have curved, reflective surfaces that focus sunlight into the centre. They can reach 204°C, which is hot enough to prepare meals.

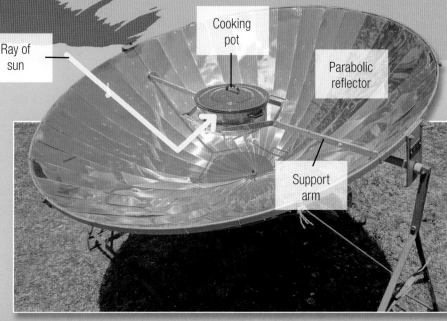

Ray of sun

Cooking pot

Parabolic reflector

Support arm

Solar cookers use a free energy source – sunlight – and are particularly useful in some of the poorest countries or in places where there is no electricity. This cooker is being used to cook food in a village high up in the mountains of Nepal.

Hot space

Look up at the night sky and you will see thousands of stars. In the heart of a living star, hydrogen atoms smash together at high speed to make heat and light. In the process they create new helium atoms. When a star dies, many of those atoms are released into space and seed new stars.

DID YOU KNOW?

In space, the hottest stars shine blue-white. The colour depends on the surface temperature and the amount of energy it emits. Our Sun is a yellow star.

Star surface temperature

30,000°C

10,000°C

5,500°C

4,000°C

3,000°C

NEBULA

Some nebulae are where stars are made, a kind of stellar nursery. A nebula is an enormous cloud of dust and hydrogen gas trillions of kilometres across. New stars form inside – a part of the cloud contracts and becomes more dense, getting hotter and eventually fusing the hydrogen to form a new star.

The Pacman Nebula is an area of active star formation 9,200 light years from Earth in the constellation Cassiopeia.

THE SUN

The Sun, our star, generates power – enough to melt a bridge of ice 3km wide and 1.5km thick stretching from Earth to the Sun in one second! Deep inside, it is fusing hydrogen atoms together to produce helium. This nuclear fusion gives off light and heat that is driven from the core towards the surface and out into space. This journey can take more than one million years!

The temperature at the Sun's core is an incredible 15 million °C.

SOLAR STORMS

The surface of the Sun is turbulent. Great storms cause giant flares to erupt and stream extra radiation and particles out through space. They can have a serious effect on Earth, interfering with satellites, electrical grids and communication systems.

HOTTEST PLANET

The second planet from the Sun, Venus, orbits it at a distance of more than 108 million kilometres. The temperature on this planet is hot enough to melt lead – more than 470°C. This is because Venus has a thick atmosphere that is made up mainly of carbon dioxide. When rays from the Sun reach Venus, their radiation is trapped by this layer, creating a runaway greenhouse effect (see page 32).

TEMPERATURES IN SPACE

The Sun's radiant energy, or rays, travel through space but do not heat it because space is almost empty. It is only when the rays hit matter – Earth, you, or anything made up of atoms – that part of the radiant energy is absorbed and heats up the object.

SUPERNOVA

Although few and far between, stars that are the most massive – eight times the size of the Sun – are able to heat their cores to several billion degrees. When one of these runs out of fuel, it collapses under its own weight and destroys itself in a huge explosion called a supernova.

The stunning Crab Nebula is the remains of a supernova.

Strange
but true

So heat is all around you – in your body, in volcanoes, in space . . . It affects every part of your life and everything you do. Here are some of the more extraordinary ways in which heat affects people and other living things on our planet.

FIERY FACT

The hottest man-made temperature ever recorded is 5.5 trillion °C – 100,000 times hotter than the Sun's interior – when scientists at CERN's Large Hadron Collider collided lead ions in 2012.

The toco toucan has an interesting way of keeping cool. Its enormous beak – about one-third of its length – helps to keep the bird cool. The toucan, like other birds, cannot sweat, so it alters the blood flow to its beak to control the amount of heat that is released or conserved.

The **black circles around meerkats' eyes** absorb the **Sun's rays** and **stop them** from **reflecting back** into their **eyes**.

SOLAR POWER

The largest solar kitchen in the world is at the Shirdi Sai Baba temple in India. The 84 rooftop-mounted reflectors help the cooks produce up to 38,500 meals in the middle of the day when the Sun is at its highest in the sky.

CHILLIES: HOT OR NOT?

In themselves they are not!
Chillies contain a chemical called
capsaicin. This stimulates nerves
in your skin and tongue to make
your brain think that they are
burning. The more chillies you
eat, the less the nerves react and
the hotter the chillies you can eat.

The hottest chilli in the world is the
Smokin Ed's 'Carolina Reaper'.

On the Spanish island of Lanzarote, off
the coast of Morocco, there is a unique
restaurant called *El Diablo* (The Devil).
The chefs there work in an extraordinary
kitchen – they cook food over heat
produced by an active volcano! A giant
grill has been installed over a cooking
pit that has nine layers of volcanic
basalt rock as a base. The volcano,
which last erupted in 1824, cooks
the food at a steady 400°C.

HOT WORK!

The hottest place of work is probably
the Mponeng gold mine, South Africa.
It is one of the deepest mines in the
world. Four kilometres below the
surface the temperature of the rock
can reach 60°C. For people to work
there, 6,000 tonnes of ice a day have
to be pumped in and refrigerated air
is blown through the passageways.

BOILING OVER

Per cubic metre, your body
makes more heat than
the Sun! The human body
creates so much heat that if,
after activity, you were able
to collect 30 minutes' worth
of heat from your entire body
you could boil water!

Roy C. Sullivan, a former park
ranger in Shenandoah National
Park, Virginia, USA, holds the
record for being struck by lightning
seven times . . . and surviving!

Hot quiz

Now you have found out what makes your everyday life and the universe hot, test your knowledge with a sizzling quiz!

1 What is heat measured by?

2 How much television can you watch if you recycle one aluminium can?

3 Which animal eats and drinks poo?

4 Why do cells in your skin produce melanin?

5 What are the biggest and most dangerous volcanoes called?

6 How much rainfall does a desert get?

7 Where are new stars born?

8 When and where was the first fire brigade established?

9 What kind of energy must be changed to stop a car?

10 What is the name of plants that take their food and drink from the air?

11 Name two things that are powered by steam.

EXTRA TOUGH QUESTIONS:

12 What are the three ways in which heat moves?

13 What is the process used to melt iron in rocks for use in industry?

14 What plants benefit from the blazing inferno of a forest fire?

15 Why is it hotter at the Equator than at the poles?

16 Which colour stars are the hottest and what temperature are they?

17 What is happening when you shiver?

1. Heat is measured by temperature (see p.9). **2.** Three hours (see p.33). **3.** The dung beetle (see p.14). **4.** Melanin helps protect the deep layers of your skin (see p.13). **5.** Stratovolcanoes (see p.25). **6.** Less than 25cm a year (see p.26). **7.** Inside a nebula (see p.36). **8.** 6ct in Rome (see p.19). **9.** Kinetic energy (see p.10). **10.** Epiphytes (see p.29). **11.** Steam trains and power stations (see p.34). **12.** Radiation, convection and conduction (see p.11). **13.** Smelting (see p.23). **14.** Fire lily and eucalyptus (see p.17). **15.** Because sunlight strikes the Earth directly at the Equator and at an angle at the poles (see p.30). **16.** Blue-white and 30,000°C (see p.36). **17.** Your muscles are rapidly contracting and generating heat to warm you up (see p.12).

Websites and further reading

Explore these websites and visit the venues for more information about the hot topics you have been reading about in the book.

- Fire in the Fire Pavilion at the Magna Science Adventure Centre, Sheffield
  www.visitmagna.co.uk/content/58/fire-pavilion

- Solar power in the Scientrific Gallery, Catalyst Science Discovery Centre, Liverpool:
  www.catalyst.org.uk/about/scientrific.htm

- Thermal imaging cameras at the Science Museum, London:
  www.sciencemuseum.org.uk/objects/interactives/launchpad/thermal%20_imaging_camera.aspx

- Steam engines at the Museum of Science and Industry, Manchester:
  www.mosi.org.uk/explore-mosi/explore-mosi-themes/energy/steam-engines.aspx

- The titan arum plant at the Royal Botanic Gardens, Kew, London:
  www.kew.org/science-conservation/plants-fungi/amorphophallus-titanum-titan-arum

- Nebulae and supernovae at the Planetarium, Bristol Science Centre, Bristol:
  www.at-bristol.org.uk/planetarium.html

- Volcanoes and earthquakes at the Natural History Museum, London:
  http://nhm.ac.uk/visit-us/galleries/red-zone/volcanoes-earthquakes/index.html

- Climate change at the Natural History Museum, London:
  www.nhm.ac.uk/nature-online/environmental-change

- Rainforests and deserts at Paignton Zoo, Devon:
  www.paigntonzoo.org.uk/animals-plants/zoo-habitats

Here are some hot books for you to explore:

- *Extreme Weather* by Thomas M. Kostigen, National Geographic Kids 2014
- *In the Shadow of the Volcano* by Caryn Jenner, Dorling Kindersley 2014
- *It's Elementary!: Putting the crackle into chemistry* by Robert Winston, Dorling Kindersley 2010
- *Night Sky* by Giles Sparrow, Scholastic 2012
- *The Vanishing Rainforest* by Richard Platt, Frances Lincoln Children's Books 2007

Glossary

asbestos
A mineral found in the ground. It has fibres and is woven into a cloth that does not burn.

asteroid
A very small world that moves around the Sun. Asteroids are found mainly between the orbits of Mars and Jupiter.

atmosphere
The layer of gases that surrounds a planet or star. Earth's atmosphere is made of air.

atom
A tiny particle of matter, consisting of protons, neutrons and electrons. Atoms are the smallest particles that can take part in a chemical reaction.

biomass
Plant material used for fuel.

canopy
The layer of rainforest between the understorey below and emergent layer above. Most rainforest animals live in the canopy.

cell
One of the tiny units that make up all living things.

combustion
The chemical reaction between a fuel and oxygen that produces heat and, usually, light.

condense
To turn a gas into a liquid. Water is condensed steam.

deforestation
The act of cutting down trees and vegetation to make room for farming or mining, or to use the wood.

digestion
The breaking down of food inside the gut so that it can be used to fuel the body.

electromagnetic
Describes a type of magnet that can be switched on and off. When it is turned on, electricity flows through a coil of wire, creating a magnetic field.

energy
The power to do work. People get energy from food. Engines get energy from fuel such as petrol.

evaporate
To change from a liquid to a gas.

flammable
Describes materials that catch fire easily.

fossil fuel
A fuel that is formed from the ancient remains of living things. Fossil fuels include coal, oil and natural gas. They contain high levels of carbon, and they release carbon dioxide when they are burned.

friction
The rubbing of one surface against another surface. Friction slows things down.

greenhouse gas
Any gas in the atmosphere that plays a part in the greenhouse effect – the trapping of heat by gases in a planet's atmosphere. The most important greenhouse gases are carbon dioxide and water vapour.

hydropower
Electricity that is generated using the power of water.

hydrothermal vent
An opening on the seafloor from which very hot, mineral-rich water flows. Also called a black smoker.

infrared
Invisible wave lengths just beyond red in the visible spectrum.

ion
An electrically charged atom or group of atoms.

kinetic energy
The amount of work an object can do as a result of its motion. The kinetic energy of a moving object depends on its mass and how fast it is moving.

microprocessor
A computer processor with microscopic electronic circuits and components.

microwave
A type of very short radio wave that travels through space. It stirs up the molecules of water in objects, making them hot.

molecule
A chemical unit made up of two or more atoms joined together.

nocturnal
Describes animals that are active during the night.

oases
Places in the desert where underground water comes to the surface and plants can grow. *Singular*: oasis

photosynthesis
The way in which plants make food. They use the energy in sunlight to turn carbon dioxide and water into sugars. Oxygen is released.

pollinate
Move pollen from one flower to another to help make seeds. Insects are the most common carriers of the pollen.

temperature
The measure of how hot or cold something is. Thermometers are used to measure temperature in degrees.

thrust
The force, usually generated by an engine, that pushes a vehicle forwards.

troposphere
The layer of air about 13km thick just above the surface of Earth.

turbine
A wheel with curved blades that is spun by the movement of a gas or a liquid. Turbines drive machines that make electricity.

virus
The tiniest type of germ. A virus takes over the cells of a living thing to make copies of itself.

ABBREVIATIONS

BCE
Before the Common Era

CE
Common Era

mya
Million years ago

ya
Years ago

Index